ALTERNATIVE ENERGY

BIOFUELS

by Kate Conley

Content Consultant
Richard M. Amasino
College of Agricultural Arts and Sciences
University of Wisconsin–Madison

Core Library

An Imprint of Abdo Publishing
abdopublishing.com

abdopublishing.com

Published by Abdo Publishing, a division of ABDO, PO Box 398166, Minneapolis, Minnesota 55439. Copyright © 2017 by Abdo Consulting Group, Inc. International copyrights reserved in all countries. No part of this book may be reproduced in any form without written permission from the publisher. Core Library™ is a trademark and logo of Abdo Publishing.

Printed in the United States of America, North Mankato, Minnesota
082016
012017

Cover Photo: Fotokostic/Shutterstock Images
Interior Photos: Fotokostic/Shutterstock Images, 1; Shutterstock Images, 4, 10, 25, 43; Jacques Palut/Shutterstock Images, 6; Valentyn Volkov/Shutterstock Images, 12; Science Source, 16, 32; Red Line Editorial, 19; Sergey Novikov/Shutterstock Images, 20; Sunny Forest/Shutterstock Images, 22, 45; David Nunuk/Science Source, 27; Martin Bond/Science Source, 29; Volker Steger/Science Source, 36; Miguel Schincariol/AFP/Getty Images, 38; Alf Ribeiro/Shutterstock Images, 40

Editor: Arnold Ringstad
Series Designer: Nikki Farinella

Publisher's Cataloging-in-Publication Data

Names: Conley, Kate, author.
Title: Biofuels / by Kate Conley.
Description: Minneapolis, MN : Abdo Publishing, 2017. | Series: Alternative
    energy | Includes bibliographical references and index.
Identifiers: LCCN 2016945413 | ISBN 9781680784534 (lib. bdg.) |
    ISBN 9781680798388 (ebook)
Subjects: LCSH: Biomass energy--Juvenile literature. | Biodiesel fuels resources--
    Juvenile literature. | Renewable energy sources--Juvenile literature.
Classification: DDC 662/.88--dc23
LC record available at http://lccn.loc.gov/2016945413

CONTENTS

FUEL OF THE FUTURE

It is a bright, sunny day in eastern Tennessee. A few puffy clouds dot the blue sky. Farmer Randall Peters looks out on his fields. He has common crops, such as corn and wheat. Tall switchgrass also sways in the breeze. The switchgrass will not be used as food. Instead, it will be made into a fuel called ethanol. The plants Peters is growing will power cars as they zoom down the highway.

Switchgrass can be used to produce biofuel.

Restaurant fryer oil is a common source of biodiesel.

A different type of fuel is being made in Atlanta, Georgia. A white tanker truck pulls up to a restaurant. The driver is not looking for a meal. She is collecting used fryer oil. Restaurants use this oil to make fried foods. Used oil usually goes to waste. Today, scientists can turn it into a fuel called biodiesel.

Ethanol and biodiesel are biofuels. A biofuel is a fuel produced by a biological process, such as plant growth. Biofuels may someday replace fossil fuels. Fossil fuels are today's most popular energy source. They include gasoline and diesel.

Fossil Fuels

Gas and diesel have been used for more than 100 years. They are efficient and powerful. Crews drill deep into the ground to find petroleum. They pump it to the surface. This substance is also called oil. It is made into gas and diesel. Almost all cars run on these fossil fuels.

Fossil fuels have downsides. Using them releases carbon dioxide. This gas traps heat in the atmosphere. These emissions lead to climate change.

Another problem is that fossil fuels are

Carbon Footprint

A carbon footprint is the amount of carbon dioxide each person is responsible for releasing into the atmosphere. About 40 percent of a person's carbon footprint comes from direct energy use. Examples of this are riding the school bus or using air conditioning. The other 60 percent comes from indirect energy use. Examples include eating food that was transported to the grocery store. People can reduce their carbon footprints. They can buy local foods. They can walk instead of drive. And they can unplug electronics when not in use.

nonrenewable. Once they are gone, they cannot be replaced. Because of these downsides, researchers are seeking new energy sources.

Biofuels

Biofuels are sources of energy that come from biomass. Biomass is living matter. This includes plants. Chemical processes change biomass into ethanol or biodiesel.

Ethanol is a clear, colorless alcohol. It makes up 70 percent of today's biofuels. Most cars cannot run on pure ethanol. It would damage the engine. For this reason, ethanol is mixed with gasoline. Most fuel is sold as E10. It is 90 percent gasoline and 10 percent ethanol.

Flex-Fuel Vehicles

Some new cars can use higher levels of ethanol. They are called flex-fuel vehicles (FFVs). FFVs can run on gasoline or a mix of ethanol and gasoline. A sensor in the car determines which fuels are in the tank. The car adjusts how the engine runs to match the fuel.

Not all engines run on gasoline or ethanol. Buses and other large vehicles often use diesel. Diesel engines are loud and dirty. For this reason, many drivers are switching to biodiesel. It burns cleaner and quieter. Biodiesel makes up 30 percent of today's biofuels.

Biofuel Benefits

Biofuels have many benefits. The first is the price. Ethanol often costs less than gasoline. When ethanol is blended with gasoline, drivers pay less.

The environment also benefits from biofuels. Like fossil fuels, they release carbon dioxide when burned. However, the plants also absorbed carbon dioxide as they grew. The total amount of carbon dioxide in the air does not increase much.

Biofuels are also safer to transport. Ethanol that spills will break down safely. If an oil tanker spills, the oil harms nearby plants and animals.

Biofuels are renewable. Crops can be replanted every year. This ensures a steady supply of energy.

Biofuel processing plants need workers for making and transporting biofuels.

Making biofuels also creates jobs. In 2015 more than 85,000 Americans worked in this industry. More workers will be needed as biofuels spread.

The Drawbacks

Biofuels have many benefits, but they are not perfect. Earth has a fixed amount of farmland. It is being filled with more energy crops. This leaves less land for food crops. Biofuel opponents fear this will reduce the food supply in the future. Food prices could increase. Farmers are looking for new places to grow crops. Biofuel critics fear farmers will cut down native plants to create fields.

Despite these drawbacks, governments are requiring more biofuels. Today biofuels make up 3.5 percent of all vehicle fuels worldwide. Experts estimate biofuels will make up 27 percent of the world's transportation fuels by 2050.

EXPLORE ONLINE

Chapter One discusses how burning fuels can release carbon dioxide into the atmosphere. Visit the website below to estimate the amount of carbon dioxide you release in a year. What can you learn from the website about how to reduce your carbon footprint?

Carbon Footprint Calculator
mycorelibrary.com/biofuels

CHAPTER TWO

THE HISTORY OF BIOFUELS

People have used biofuels for thousands of years. They made wood fires to keep warm. They made oil lamps from shells. The shells were filled with moss soaked in animal fat. The moss was then lit on fire.

Early in US history, wood was the most important biofuel. It was plentiful and easy to transport. People used wood to heat their homes and cook. On the

Wood has been a common and easily available biofuel throughout human history.

prairies, wood was scarce. Settlers turned to other biofuels. They burned dried cow droppings, corncobs, and sunflower stalks.

People used biofuels for lighting too. Early lamps were fueled by whale oil. In the 1820s people began using camphene. It was a mix of alcohol, turpentine, and camphor. Camphene was cheap. It made a bright flame and gave off little smoke. It quickly became the biofuel Americans preferred.

By 1860 creating alcohol for fuel was a large industry. Every year, American distilleries made 90 million gallons (340 million L) for lamps alone. Farmers could use stills to make their own alcohol fuel. They fermented crops and other plant waste.

War and Taxes

The American Civil War (1861–1865) changed the nation's use of biofuels. The war was expensive. To raise money, leaders passed a tax on alcohol in 1862. At first it was 20 cents per gallon (3.8 L). By 1864 taxes had risen to $2.08 per gallon. This is equal to about $30 per gallon in today's money.

Sales of alcohol fuels dropped quickly. Buyers turned to kerosene. It is a liquid fuel made from petroleum. Kerosene was cheap and burned brightly. It had a lower tax too. Kerosene soon replaced alcohol fuels.

Diesel and Ford

In the 1890s, German engineer Rudolf Diesel designed a new type of engine. It was more efficient than existing steam engines. It was also more reliable than gasoline engines. It had another unusual feature too. It could run on vegetable oil.

Experiments with Ethanol

Inventors turned to alcohol to fuel engines too. Around 1826, American Samuel Morey created an engine that used ethanol and turpentine. Morey's engine powered a wagon and a small boat. In Germany, Nicholas Otto made an ethanol-powered engine in 1860. Morey and Otto's engines worked well, but neither one had widespread success. They could not find investors. People at the time preferred steam engines.

The engine technology developed by Rudolf Diesel more than 100 years ago is still in use today.

The public saw a biofuel engine in 1900. That year, France hosted the World's Fair. The new technology was displayed at the fair. French leaders asked scientists to make a peanut oil engine. They hoped to use peanut oil as a fuel in their African colonies. The oil was a good source of energy. The engine was a success.

American automaker Henry Ford also believed in biofuels. In 1906 Congress removed the alcohol tax. Ethanol was affordable again. Ford used it for his Model T car. The Model T went on sale in 1908. It could run on ethanol, gasoline, or a mix of the two.

Fossil Fuels Take Over

While Diesel and Ford worked on their engines, a new era was beginning. In October 1900, miners

Rudolf Diesel

Rudolf Diesel was a German engineer. He created an engine in 1897. It brought him wealth and fame. Diesel felt strongly about using biofuels in it. In 1912 he said,

The diesel engine can be fed with vegetable oils and would help considerably in the development of agriculture of the countries which use it. The use of vegetable oils for engine fuels may seem insignificant today. But such oils may become in course of time as important as petroleum and the coal tar products of the present time.

drilled for petroleum at Spindletop Hill in Texas. On January 10, 1901, oil began gushing 150 feet (46 m) in the air. It was the largest oil well ever seen. It produced 100,000 barrels of oil a day.

The Spindletop oil started the US fossil fuel boom. Miners formed new companies. They drilled wells across Texas. Oil was cheap, plentiful, and powerful. Fossil fuels replaced biofuels.

By the 1970s, oil was the top US energy source. US companies began to import oil from other nations. Much of the supply came from the Organization of the Petroleum Exporting Countries (OPEC). OPEC included the Middle-Eastern nations of Saudi Arabia, Kuwait, and Libya.

The Oil Crisis

At first, buying oil from OPEC worked fine. But its members disliked US policies in the Middle East. OPEC put an embargo on oil it sold to the United States in 1973. Prices skyrocketed. Oil went from $3

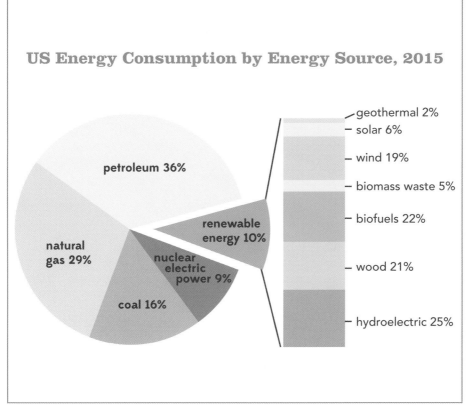

US Energy Consumption by Energy Source, 2015

- petroleum 36%
- natural gas 29%
- nuclear electric power 9%
- coal 16%
- renewable energy 10%

- geothermal 2%
- solar 6%
- wind 19%
- biomass waste 5%
- biofuels 22%
- wood 21%
- hydroelectric 25%

US Energy Consumption in 2015

This graph shows the energy sources used by the United States in 2015. Biofuels still make up a relatively small percentage of US energy. What sources are used more, and which are used less? How do you think this graph might look different in 10 years? How might it look in 50 years?

a barrel to $12 a barrel. Gas stations ran out of fuel. People who could find gasoline paid high prices.

The embargo ended in 1974. Gas prices dropped. People used more oil in the 1980s and 1990s. Many government leaders were worried. They did not

19

Most of today's cars still run on fuels made from oil. But biofuels are becoming more popular.

want to rely on other nations for oil. There were other reasons not to use oil too. Scientists began to warn people about the dangers of burning oil. It was polluting the environment.

Americans began to look into biofuels. In 2005 Congress passed the Renewable Fuel Standard Program (RFSP). It set standards for how much renewable fuel the country should use. Each year, the RFSP states, biofuels are supposed to be used more.

In the fall of 1925, Henry Ford spoke about the future of energy. Many others at the time were focused on fossil fuels. Ford believed the future of energy would come from biomass:

> *The fuel of the future is going to come from fruit like that sumac out by the road, or from apples, weeds, sawdust—almost anything. There is fuel in every bit of vegetable matter that can be fermented. There is enough alcohol in one year's yield of an acre of potatoes to drive the machinery necessary to cultivate the field for one hundred years.*

> Source: "Ford Predicts Fuel from Vegetation." New York Times. *New York Times,* September 20, 1925. Web. Accessed April 22, 2016.

Changing Minds

Imagine you take the same views as Ford, but your best friend believes fossil fuels are the future of energy. Write an e-mail to your friend explaining your position. Include facts to support your ideas. What benefits of biofuels does Ford describe?

CHAPTER THREE

MAKING BIOFUELS

Biofuels can power many vehicles. Bulldozers, flex-fuel cars, and school buses can all run on biofuels. No matter what they power, all biofuels begin in the same way. They start with sunlight.

Earth's plants take in the sun's energy. This process is called photosynthesis. Plants use sunlight to

The sun is the original source of energy for all types of biofuels.

create oxygen and carbohydrates. Plants are the basic building blocks of all biofuels.

Plants provide fuel in many ways. When eating an apple, a person's body breaks it down into sugars. Then the body uses these sugars for energy. The same basic process happens in the production of biofuels. First the plants are broken down into flour. Then scientists add different substances to break down the plants further.

One such substance is yeast. It is a fungus that eats sugar. When it is added to ground corn and water, it eats the corn's sugars. The yeast turns the sugar into ethanol. To make biodiesel, scientists use catalysts. Catalysts speed up chemical reactions. When mixed with alcohol, catalysts help break down oils into biodiesel.

Making Ethanol

In the United States, approximately 90 percent of ethanol is made by dry milling. To dry mill ethanol, the first step is grinding the corn into flour. Workers

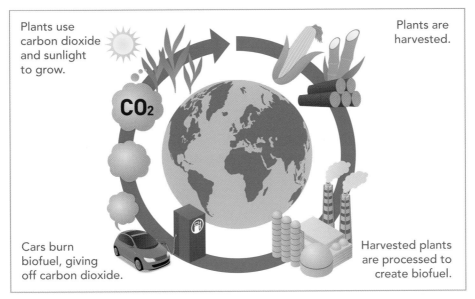

Plants use carbon dioxide and sunlight to grow.

Plants are harvested.

CO_2

Cars burn biofuel, giving off carbon dioxide.

Harvested plants are processed to create biofuel.

Biofuels and Carbon Dioxide

The plants grown for biofuels consume carbon dioxide as they grow. This helps offset the carbon dioxide produced when the biofuels are used. Using biofuels rather than fossil fuels can lead to a healthier environment. How could other alternative fuels make this cycle even better for the Earth?

then add water and an enzyme. The resulting mixture is called mash. Jets of steam heat the mash to temperatures above 212 degrees Fahrenheit (100°C). As the mash cools, another enzyme is added. This process converts the corn's starch into sugar.

Once the mash is completely cooled, workers transfer it to large tanks called fermenters. They add yeast to convert the corn's sugar into alcohol. This part of the process takes approximately two full days. After being fermented, the mash goes into distillers. There the alcohol is separated from the rest of the mash.

Next, workers dehydrate the alcohol. This removes leftover water. It leaves pure alcohol and makes the fuel more powerful. The final step is adding a small amount of gasoline to the ethanol. This makes it poisonous to drink, ensuring it will not be taxed as a beverage.

Making Biodiesel

Like ethanol, biodiesel is created through

The Biofuels Corridor

In 2006 the US Department of Energy provided $1.3 million to create the Biofuels Corridor on Interstate 65. This highway stretches 886 miles (1,426 km) from Lake Michigan to the Gulf of Mexico. It passes through Indiana, Kentucky, Tennessee, and Alabama. Biofuel filling stations line the way. Drivers on the route are never more than a quarter tank away from the nearest station. This highway is the first of its kind in the United States. It makes biofuel vehicles practical for many drivers.

Workers take samples during the ethanol production process to check the fuel's quality.

chemistry. It begins with the energy source, which is a fat or an oil. Soybeans produce approximately 50 percent of the biodiesel made in the United States. Canola oil, corn oil, animal fats, and fryer oil make up the rest.

The first step in the process is mixing a catalyst, usually lye, with an alcohol, commonly methanol. This mixture is added to a tank of oil or fat. It is heated and stirred for several hours. This process converts the fat or oil into biodiesel and glycerol.

The glycerol and biodiesel must be separated. For the next 24 hours, gravity does the work. The honey-colored

Biofuel By-Products

When factories make biofuels, other products are also created. They are called by-products. To make ethanol, factories use only the corn's starch. The remaining parts of the corn can be put to other uses. Farmers feed them to cows, chickens, and pigs. When creating biodiesel, a liquid called glycerin forms. Refined glycerin can be used in soap, medicine, and makeup.

People can put biodiesel and other biofuels in their cars at many normal filling stations.

biodiesel rises to the top of the tank. The glycerol sinks to the bottom. Sometimes the separation needs to happen sooner. Workers can put the mixture into a centrifuge. This machine spins rapidly. It separates the biodiesel and glycerol.

Next, the biodiesel is put into a distiller. There, the alcohol is removed. The biodiesel is sprayed with water. It is allowed to settle. Any remaining lye or glycerol sinks to the bottom of the tank with the water. The result is a pure, safe, liquid fuel.

Biofuel Blends

Most diesel engines made after the 1970s can run on 100 percent biodiesel (B100). Cold weather can bring problems, though. Temperatures below 45 degrees Fahrenheit (7°C) thicken B100. This stops engines from working.

To prevent this, scientists mix biodiesel with fossil fuels. Fossil fuels have a lower freezing point than biodiesel. This prevents it from thickening. A common winter blend is B20. It is 20 percent biodiesel and 80 percent fossil fuels. It allows snowplows, tow trucks, buses, and other vehicles to run smoothly in winter.

In 2016 US secretary of agriculture Tom Vilsack spoke about biofuels in an interview:

> *The reality is the biofuel industry has allowed consumers in this country to have less expensive gas, anywhere from 25 cents to a dollar [per gallon], depending on the price of gas at any given point in time, saved as a result of the biofuel industry. It helps to employ, directly or indirectly, over 4,000 folks. It's stabilized farm prices and it has taken, in the last 15 years, the equivalent to 124 million cars off the road. So there are many benefits to this industry, and it provides for less reliance on foreign oil, which is one of the reasons why we are now in a position to be less reliant on foreign oil than we were 10 or 15 years ago.*

Source: "U.S. Agriculture Secretary Talks GMOs and Ethanol." Here & Now. Trustees of Boston University, February 25, 2016. Web. Accessed April 22, 2016.

What's the Big Idea?

Imagine you are writing a blog entry to convince people to build more biofuel processing plants. Use the facts in the quote by Tom Vilsack to support your ideas.

CHAPTER FOUR

THE FUTURE OF BIOFUELS

When people think of biofuels, they often think of corn, sugarcane, or soybeans. Fuels are made directly from these plants' sugars, starches, or oils. They are referred to as first-generation biofuels.

Scientists are now looking into new types of biofuel. One of those types would be made from by-products of first-generation biofuels.

Biofuel researchers are developing new ways to unlock the power of plant-based fuels.

This type is known as a second-generation biofuel. It increases the amount of energy a single plant can provide. Switchgrass is one common source of second-generation biofuel. These fuels may be the future of the biofuel industry.

Cellulosic Ethanol

Many scientists are looking to cellulose as a future source of ethanol. It is the most abundant organic compound on Earth. Every living plant produces cellulose. It is the woody substance that allows plants to stay upright. Accessing the

Surprising Uses for Biodiesel

People have used biodiesel mostly for fueling vehicles. Scientists are exploring other ways to use biodiesel in the future. When tankers spill oil in the ocean, for example, biodiesel is a safe and effective cleaning agent. Engineers are designing new generators that can run on 100 percent biodiesel. This will allow power plants to produce clean electricity. Biodiesel can even clean greasy tools and engine parts, make gears run smoothly, and stop bike chains from squeaking.

energy stored in cellulose is expensive and difficult. This has stopped people from making ethanol out of it in the past.

New processes are making cellulosic ethanol a reality. The most difficult part is breaking down the cellulose into sugar. To do this, plants are soaked in water and chemicals. Next, fungi are added. They eat dead plant matter. This process creates enzymes that break down the cellulose. The resulting sugar can then be converted into ethanol.

In late 2012 the world's first large-scale cellulosic ethanol factory opened in Italy. It uses reeds, rice straw, and wheat straw to make ethanol. In 2015 three US factories began making cellulosic ethanol. They use parts of crops that are left after harvest. These parts include corncobs, cornhusks, and cornstalks.

Algae

Cellulose is just one of the new biofuels of the future. Some scientists are looking to completely new sources, such as algae. These are tiny, fast-growing

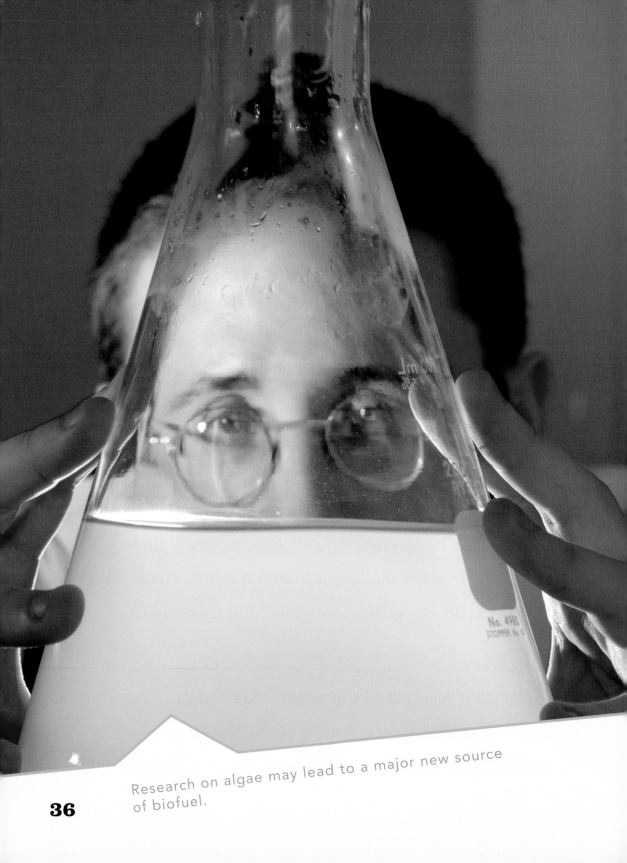

Research on algae may lead to a major new source of biofuel.

water plants. Many types of algae store energy as oil. Algae can produce more oil than any land-based plant.

To access the oil, scientists need to break down the cell wall. They are experimenting with how to do this. Some use sound waves to break down the cells. Others put dried algae into a press. This breaks the cells and squeezes out the oil. Chemicals can also be added to algae to break down the cells. Once the oil is harvested, it can be processed like any other biodiesel.

The environment benefits from algae biofuel too. Algae use carbon dioxide to grow. This offsets the amount of carbon dioxide released when algal oil is used as fuel.

A Biofuel Model

As countries strive to use more biofuels in the future, they often look to Brazil as an example. Brazil's biofuel story began in 1973. That year, gas prices skyrocketed

Machinery moves sugarcane material into a cellulosic ethanol plant in Brazil.

across the globe. Brazilian leaders wanted new energy options. One of those was ethanol.

Brazil invested in sugarcane farms. This crop grew well in Brazil. It could also be turned into ethanol easily. The government built ethanol factories.

It required Brazil's cars to have flex-fuel engines. All gasoline had to be blended with ethanol.

The results in Brazil have been staggering. The country no longer relies on other countries for its power. Thanks to its vast farmland, warm growing climate, and relatively small energy needs, Brazil is completely energy independent.

Drawbacks and Goals

Though Brazil is a model for the future of biofuels, it is not perfect. Critics fear expanding sugarcane fields will push other farmers and ranchers to clear forests. Converting

The Power of Bagasse

When sugarcane is made into ethanol, only one-third of the sugarcane's energy ends up in the fuel. The remaining two-thirds is locked in the sugarcane's stalk. The ground-up stalk is called bagasse. This ethanol by-product has many uses. Bagasse can be burned to produce electricity. Many of Brazil's sugar mills are powered by the bagasse they create. Bagasse can also be used to make cellulosic ethanol, animal feed, paper, and plastics.

Brazil's biofuel industry has succeeded in supplying a large portion of the nation's energy needs.

these areas into fields will hurt native plants and animals.

Critics also worry about pollution related to ethanol. Water used to process the sugarcane into ethanol is drained into local rivers. It can pollute them. Farmers usually burn their fields after harvesting sugarcane. This creates air pollution.

Despite these drawbacks, it appears Brazil can teach the world many lessons about biofuels. A nation does not have to rely mainly on fossil fuels for power. Biofuels can play an important role in satisfying energy needs. But this is not an easy change to make. It takes commitment from leaders in business, government, and science. Increasingly, nations across the globe are striving for the goal that Brazil has achieved. It has become clear that biofuels will be an important part of our energy future.

FURTHER EVIDENCE

Chapter Four discusses the future of biofuels. People agree that fossil fuels will someday run out. But not everyone agrees that biofuels are the solution to the world's energy problems. The article at the link below discusses the drawbacks to biofuels. Does the article support the ideas present in Chapter Four? Why or why not?

Biofuels Do More Harm Than Good?
mycorelibrary.com/biofuels

FAST FACTS

- The two main types of biofuels are ethanol and biodiesel.
- Ethanol makes up 70 percent of all biofuels. The two main crops used to make ethanol are corn and sugarcane.
- Biodiesel makes up 30 percent of all biofuels. Vegetable oils, animal fats, and waste oil are the main sources of biodiesel.
- Producing biofuels creates jobs. It also gives nations greater energy independence.
- People have been using ethanol and biodiesel to power engines for more than 100 years.
- Scientists are experimenting with new sources for biofuels, such as algae and cellulose.
- Some critics of biofuels worry that making fuels out of crops will cause food shortages.
- Brazil has used biofuels to become completely energy independent.

- Flex-fuel vehicles give drivers the power to choose what types of fuels they use: either gasoline or a blend of ethanol and gasoline.

Take a Stand

Chapter Four discusses Brazil's experiences with biofuels. After the oil embargo of 1973, Brazil's government focused on using biofuels to make their nation energy independent. Is this a good idea? Are there any drawbacks to this plan? Write a paragraph explaining your opinions.

You Are There

Chapter Three explains how biofuels are made. Imagine you are an artist who travels to a biofuel production plant. When you are done with your tour, you must make a poster showing the process. What does your presentation look like? Use bright colors, simple graphics, and short phrases to explain how ethanol or biodiesel is made.

Dig Deeper

Chapter Four discusses the future of biofuels, especially new sources of fuel. Ask a librarian to help you find articles about two other sources of renewable fuel. How do these sources compare to what you have learned about biofuels?

Say What?

Studying energy technologies can involve learning many new words. Look through the book's text and find five new words you did not know. Look up the definitions in a dictionary. Write five sentences using the new words you have learned.

GLOSSARY

carbohydrate
sugar, starch, and cellulose
made by green plants

dehydrate
to remove water from
another substance, such as
food or fuel

distillery
a place where a substance is
changed into alcohol

embargo
a stop in trade between
groups

emission
a substance released into
the air

enzyme
a protein that starts a
chemical reaction

import
to bring a product from one
nation to another

photosynthesis
a process through which
green plants use sunlight,
water, and carbon dioxide to
make energy

still
a piece of equipment used to
create alcohol

LEARN MORE

Books

Gore, Al. *Our Choice: How We Can Solve the Climate Crisis*. New York: Viking Children's Books, 2009.

Heos, Bridget. *It's Getting Hot in Here: The Past, Present, and Future of Climate Change*. Boston, MA: Houghton Mifflin Harcourt, 2015.

Newman, Patricia. *Biofuels*. Ann Arbor, MI: Cherry Lake Publishing, 2013.

Websites

To learn more about Alternative Energy, visit **booklinks.abdopublishing.com**. These links are routinely monitored and updated to provide the most current information available.

Visit **mycorelibrary.com** for free additional tools for teachers and students.

INDEX

ABOUT THE AUTHOR

Kate Conley is the author of more than 20 nonfiction books for young readers. She lives in Minnesota with her husband and two children.